DARE TO BE A UNICORN

Victoria Brock

Copyright © 2023 by Trient Press

All rights reserved. No part of this publication may be reproduced, distributed, or transmitted in any form or by any means, including photocopying, recording, or other electronic or mechanical methods, without the prior written permission of the publisher, except in the case of brief quotations embodied in critical reviews and certain other noncommercial uses permitted by copyright law. For permission requests, write to the publisher, addressed "Attention: Permissions Coordinator," at the address below.

Criminal copyright infringement, including infringement without monetary gain, is investigated by the FBI and is punishable by up to five years in federal prison and a fine of $250,000.

Except for the original story material written by the author, all songs, song titles, and lyrics mentioned in the novel Dare To Be A Unicorn are the exclusive property of the respective artists, songwriters, and copyright holder.

Trient Press
3375 S Rainbow Blvd
#81710, SMB 13135
Las Vegas,NV 89180

Ordering Information:
Quantity sales. Special discounts are available on quantity purchases by corporations, associations, and others. For details, contact the publisher at the address above.
Orders by U.S. trade bookstores and wholesalers. Please contact Trient Press: Tel: (775) 996-3844; or visit www.trientpress.com.

Printed in the United States of America

Publisher's Cataloging-in-Publication data
Brock, Victoria
A title of a book : Dare to be a Unicorn

ISBN
Hard Cover   979-8-88990-161-7
Paper Back   979-8-88990-162-4
Ebook   979-8-88990-163-1

Contents

Prologue
Mother, Mother
On Your Marks, Get Ready, Motherhood
Mommy Needs Meds
Where's My Baby
There's My Baby
Raising The Baby
Burying The Baby
Not Just A Mother's Story
What Is Work
Knowing Myself
My Mother and I
Parenting and Personhood
Discourse-Oriented Parenting
Contextualizing Authority
Moving Down South
Crowded Alone
Control and Care
Issues and Issues
A Throwback About Throwing Back
Attempting To Adjust
Double The Loneliness
Losing Your Why
Fed-Up Value
Mind, Body, Spirit
Epilogue

Prologue

Human behavior can be fascinating for all the contradictions it presents. One such anomaly is the fact that we are self-interested yet remain curious about others. Most people satisfy this curiosity by reading up celebrity gossip, watching reality TV, and even prodding into their friends' personal lives. My life has been peppered with such obstacles that I never found time for any of these things.

I had challenges to deal with, and rough patches that could have become pits had I not kept going. Looking back, I can see that my journey presents a more valuable account than most celebrity gossip and tabloid content out there. With that said, not everyone wants to satisfy their curiosity while improving themselves simultaneously. If you're reading this, chances are, you are interested in improving yourself. And for that, I applaud you. This book will be a dose of motivation, and each chapter will have the potential to spark an idea that might change your life. Turn this page so we can take this trip together.

Mother Mother

Life has a poetic way of mirroring certain themes across time. They say that tough days build character. In my case, this character-building started when I was quite young. I had a mom who had her own problems. She was verbally abusive, and despite being an okay mother (at least in my estimation), she let her personal problems bleed into my upbringing. I made a note of this as a young adult and made sure I did not make her mistakes with my own kids, but that's a story for another time.

It all started with alcohol in her case. Of course, in our culture, drinking socially is fine, and no one bats an eye if you need a little booze to have fun. It is only when someone gets too drunk too often that we realize that there is a problem. Alcohol is normalized because we don't want others to tell us how much we can drink. But if we are objective about it, we must acknowledge that it is harder to get off of than many hard drugs.

Many hard drugs one can quit cold turkey at least with proper restraint. Quitting alcohol cold turkey can actually kill you. Safe drinking campaigns help raise awareness about this, but I was born way before yesterday, and that means there wasn't a lot of such awareness back then.

As a result, many people didn't realize when they were going from casual drinkers to alcoholics. And my mother was one of them. She became an obligate drinker and eventually even graduated to other drugs. If there is supply and you're an alcoholic, chances are you'll go for something else as well. Of course, I did not know this as a young girl.

But if you're reading this and have a relative or a friend who has alcohol issues, you would be wise to move them to an environment where drugs are hard to obtain. It is not pretty what alcoholism can do to a person but combine drugs, and you have the recipe for health and financial disaster. It also creates significant problems among the children in the household; we just don't realize them at the moment. That's why, if not for the sake of this generation, then for the sake of the next, we must make sure alcohol is used moderately, and help is given often when it is required.

I decided as a young adult that I'll never make the mistakes my mother made. I tried my best to be moderate with alcohol. I will have me a good bottle of wine to unwind from time to time and if I'm at a function I might have a drink, but what I do on a daily to ease my mind and help dream land come is my Mary and I mentally prepared myself to be a discourse-oriented parent. At this point, you might be wondering what a discourse-oriented parent is. There are two types of parents: discourse-oriented and authority-oriented. Authority-centric moms will use their physical dominance to get the child to submit to discipline. Discourse-oriented parents take a longer route but get the child to ultimately decide it is in his best interest to behave. And that's what I was ready for when I first got pregnant. But life had something else in store for me.

On Your Marks, Get Ready, Motherhood

I was so excited when I first got pregnant because the man I was with was supportive and wanted to be a father. I had seen instances where women got pregnant, but the men were either reluctantly going along or not interested in being around at all. My first baby's father was interested in raising him with me and even had his family interested in the process. They would ask about me and how the baby was coming along whenever they called. He and I had a vision regarding what we wanted life to be with our baby in the picture.

But at the same time, I didn't know what to expect. The thing about being a mother the first time is that you've been a mother zero times before that. And that meant there was some nervousness that came with the excitement. But joining baby college was one of the best decisions regarding that.

Baby college might sound like a college that babies go to, but it is actually an educational program for expecting moms. Considering that this was over a decade ago in New York City, the equivalent program in your region today might not have the same name. However, programs for expecting parents are quite common.

The one I enrolled in was a weekly session and happened every Saturday, keeping me well occupied. I learned about how to manage my pregnancy and what to expect in the initial months of childcare. I was honestly quite excited about this. I would take the class and then visit the baby's father, and we would talk about what I learned, among other things.

One such Saturday, I visited him after the baby college session, and we started talking. The conversation went a couple of different tangents, and before we knew it, we were in bed together. We had sex, and I realized I was bleeding. This got me quite anxious. He was nervous, too, and we immediately checked with the doctors. They said that everything was fine and that even my water was intact.

My bleeding was a result of slight dilation, which meant that we could expect the baby soon. I was admitted right away in the maternity ward, and all around me, I could hear moms screaming in what I am told was the pleasing agony of childbirth. I didn't want to go through that kind of pleasure if it meant screaming my vocal cords off of my throat. But I was also excited. I couldn't wait to meet my baby, and I kept waiting for the rush that comes with the need to contract, and it never came.

Mommy Needs Meds

I asked the nurse why I wasn't feeling anything. She smiled and calmly told me that it was normal. She said that some mothers were natural flowers while others required assistance. She seemed to genuinely believe what she was saying, so I didn't bother pushing it or being skeptical.

Eventually, they realized this wasn't standard delivery and ran a quick check. After that, the doctor came in and, in quite a contained manner, explained that what I had was not a natural delivery procedure but nothing too rare for me to worry about. They told me that I was 6 cm dilated but not exceeding that naturally. At this pace, they believed I wouldn't go into labor anytime soon yet would be dilated to the point where life wouldn't be practical.

The standard solution in such cases is a dose of Pitocin. Pitocin is an injection featuring Oxytocin. And That's supposed to induce labor. If it doesn't, then a C-section is in order. That said, the doctors made it abundantly clear that they did not want to take that route if vaginal birth was possible.

They preferred vaginal birth probably because it is healthiest but also because they don't have to do as much of the work. When they gave me a Pitocin injection, I felt my stomach clench but didn't feel a single contraction. To this day, I don't know what a natural contraction feels like.

I was getting slightly worried because there were no signs of there being any issues with my pregnancy prior to this. I went to college and took all the doctor's appointments required. In each one, I was told the pregnancy was coming along just fine. This was the first time I had required injection and still wasn't going into labor.

As soon as I was injected with Pitocin, I had crossed the threshold. So now I sit and wait for the action to happen. The action I was expecting is not exactly what I got. BEEP BEEP BEEP is all I heard. I looked over at the heart monitor and my baby's heart rate went down, dangerously low. In a blink of an eye my room was full of nurses. At this point my son's father was just coming back in the room. **Now they had to perform a C-section, and I was taken for an emergency C-section. You can't have a baby in your womb for long after Oxytocin is in your blood and your body isn't rejecting the baby. Of course, I can't tell you much about my C-Section experience,** but what I do remember was being told to breath in and count backwards from ten to one and boom **I had passed out.**

I remember waking up groggy, and since I remembered I was in a maternity ward, I wanted to see the baby. I had my baby's father, his **father's mother,** and my grandmother aka Granny **by my side. It was sweet to have** both my Granny and **the child's grandmother there even if my mom wasn't able to get there on such short notice. "Where's my son?" I asked, and both his father and mother said, "He's asleep." As I said earlier, the thing about being a first-time mother is that you've been a mother zero times before. I had no idea that this wasn't normal. I genuinely believed that it was okay for my baby to be asleep, out of my sight.**

Where's My Baby

I kept asking the baby's father where my baby was, and he assured me he was asleep. Of course, this couldn't go on forever. One of my close friends dropped by, and she, too, was playing along. I thought for a moment why they had all seen my baby, and I hadn't. My anxiety was beginning to creep up as I started wondering whether something was wrong.

I tried to get into a festive mood because I was a fresh mom plus my birthday was a month away. While I tried to celebrate, I could clearly see my friend and my granny trying to get my mind off my son. His father, however, didn't seem too comfortable keeping me in the dark for long. I turned to him and said, "Can you just take a picture of him and show me? I wanna see him even if he's sleeping."

"I already did," he smiled, pulling out his phone. He showed me a picture of my son. Perhaps I should say that he showed me a picture of my son's back. If things were weird before, then this just explained it. Something was definitely wrong. *'Is there something wrong with his face?'* I wondered, but that was my baby. No matter how he looked, I'd love him. It didn't make sense why a son's face was hidden from his mother.

At this point, the closest I had gotten to the baby was through the man, so I asked him, "Why can't I see his face?" I don't know if it's good or bad, but he told me the truth. "He was twitching like a lot and even foaming at the mouth, so you know they couldn't..." his voice trailed off as my friend's death stare froze him. *'Why would you say that?'* she tried to telepathically convey to him. He got the message. So did I. My baby wasn't healthy.

I knew that if I wanted to get more honesty, it wouldn't be wise to freak out. I had to demonstrate to the people around me that I could handle reality. I used every ounce of strength in me to avoid bursting into tears. The next day I was visited by a doctor from the NICU and was finally told the truth about what was going on with my son and, with a controlled tone, asked, "Will he die?"

"Perhaps," said the doctor. I still didn't let my emotions take control. "Then, I want to see him," I said. "He can't come into this world and pass away without me meeting him," I explained. The doctors and everyone else in the room understood that logic. So they put me in a wheelchair and carted me to the area where they had my child.

There's My Baby

When I saw the babies in that room, all of them in incubators, I could tell which one was mine. That's because most of the babies there were prematurely born. Generally, premature babies need to be kept on some sort of a support system till they're ready to be taken to the real world. In fact, human babies are pretty much the only mammal offspring that come out of the womb not ready.

A baby calf starts walking minutes after birth. A human child needs two years because even at nine months, we're born unprepared. Premature babies, therefore, are more vulnerable, but my child wasn't born before the expected date. He was significantly larger than everyone else, 10lbs 11.6 oz to be exact. That's right I had a whole linebacker. Because my baby was the size he was he couldn't fit in an incubator so he was on something called a warmer in the ward yet still was in a similar incubator because of his condition.

I was told he had a condition called Hypoxic-ischemic encephalopathy or for short HIE. HIE is a type of newborn brain damage caused by oxygen deprivation and limited blood flow. HIE is a type of birth injury; this is a broad term used to refer to any harm that a baby experiences at or near the time of birth. When I rolled my wheelchair next to him, I could see that he wasn't crying. He was breathing so fast like he had just come from running a race. He had all kinds of tubes coming and going to and from all different places, but he was alive. The doctors said his organs were working and that somehow his mind couldn't command his body to act in the instinctual manner that babies do. So in a nut shell my son's brain wasn't sending signals for him to swallow, blink, talk and so on.

I wanted to cry, but I held back my tears. It took everything in me to hold back my tears because of how strong the urge was. However, I had to be strong for my baby. So I talked to him. I told him to relax. I kept saying, "Hey son, relax," over and over. I didn't know what to do. I couldn't touch him; they had forbidden it. I could only talk, and what could I have said. All my energy was going towards holding back tears. If I spent any energy thinking about what else to say, I would have cried.

It felt so unfair. It felt like I was given a gift and first forbidden from seeing it, and when I fought tooth and nail to get to see it, I was told I couldn't have it. I wanted it so much. I wanted him so much.

He was damn near 10 lbs, most the other babies in the NICU were premature so my sweet hunnie baby looked like he was ready to get up and go home. Due to his size when other parents would come visit their baby I would often get the question of "How old is your baby?" or "How long has he been there?" and when they got the answer of "He is a newborn." they were shocked. They just couldn't believe it. **It seemed so uncanny that he wasn't** crying or moving around like the other babies . I felt alone despite there being people around me. Who could I share my pain with; they could only understand it from a distance. They didn't know how I felt. Soon after that, they rolled me out of the room.

"We need to conduct an X-ray," they said. I had a feeling something was wrong because one of the first things I had said upon coming to my senses after the delivery was, "I'm not going to have another baby; this hurts too much." I didn't find out then what was wrong, but they actually thought they had lost an instrument in my body when doing the C-section. They even cut me open again and looked around. When they didn't find anything, they sowed me back up.

Raising The Baby

When they said my baby wasn't sure to die, a pessimistic part of me thought they were telling me a comfortable lie. However, to my relief, they were right. The baby could survive but would require to be in a long term care facility because he would need 24-hr nursing care So I had to raise my baby while he depended on modern technology to survive.

They often say that no matter what happens in your life, you learn to live with it. And at our lowest point, this might sound untrue but looking back; we realize that we've survived tougher times. I had started taking care of my child while he couldn't blink, suck or cry, and I didn't do this alone. He was at multiple hospitals across his lifetime. I visited him every day. Very grateful for my son having health insurance at the time because those hospital bills whew chile they get pricey.

His first birthday was at a hospital. My Love Bug was able to come home for a weekend visit from one of the hospitals he was in. Even tho he had to come with all the complicated machinery It didnt' matter to me not one bit. I had been praying for this moment since he was born to be able to lay next to him and listen to his heart beat. Ultimately he spent most of his life in a long term care facility. It is tough to describe the feeling because so many contradictions work together to present a mix we call our life experience. I felt helpless because I couldn't do more, but I felt empowered doing the most I could. I felt happy that I had a son, but I felt hurt knowing he wasn't experiencing everything life had to offer. I felt loved in all the support I got from those who cared about us, but I also felt alone because not one other person could truly feel what I was going through.

Most of the pain and hurt came from what I had expected motherhood to be and what it had been for me. My childhood was far from ideal, and I was so passionate about making sure my kids' childhood was going to be better. I had hoped to be a great mother, but it turned out that being a good mom doesn't always translate to granting the best childhood.

You will have moments in your life where it feels like no matter how hard you push; you will not get what you want. In those moments, you can rationalize giving up. But if you give up, you'll never know how good things could have been. A part of you will always wonder what would have been different had you kept going. I was committed to the idea of giving my best. Even if my baby wasn't going to be up and running like other kids, I was going to give it my best shot.

burying the baby

The chapter title gives away the story's end, so there's no point building up to it: my child passed away after eleven years. He was raised in hospitals and was a fighter. I still remember the moment doctors decided to tell me something was wrong. The doctor looked so sad. There's a life expectancy score that babies receive at birth. It goes from 1 to 10, with 10 showing the highest chances of survival.

My baby didn't even have one on his score. He was rated 0 out of 10 on the Apgar scale and yet managed to live 11 more years than modern medicine had predicted.

I uprooted my life in New York and moved to North Carolina so that my son and I could be together not in a hospital setting. Why move? Well i had a conversation with my sons social worker and i was told he could come home but the home would for sure require certain thiings that New York apartments just dont have. But I knew North Carolina, would be not to expensive, and I would be able to find a decent size place because space was definitely one of the many things needed. I had hopes for him like any mother has of her kids. And he managed to cross the decade line and passed soon after we moved to North Carolina.

I mourned the loss because as technically exhausting it is to raise a child with medical complications, your love grows the more you invest in your child's wellbeing. By investment, I refer to the time and emotion that goes into the process. On the surface, everyone who knew the story seemed to have empathy, but there's a level of empathy that only comes from experience, and I doubt anyone could truly understand what I went through.

To them, I was raising a child who needed life-support and critical medical supervision most of the time. They didn't see that the child was having an impact on the world. Our view of impact is so skewed. We need to see people act physically or have a material impact to believe they are leaving a mark on this world.

Nobody saw how this child made me stronger. He taught me how to be patient. He made me a better mother. He taught me how to count my blessings. I remember asking him to relax and be strong the first time I met him, but in the end, he was the one who ended up making me stronger. Sure, I put in my time, energy, and emotions, but to me, he gave me a lot more than I ever could give him,

Perhaps he had been in more hospitals in those 11 years than I had been in my whole life, but he never invited pity. You couldn't look at him and feel sorry. You could only look at him and be proud because he was the living example of the strength of human will. And for that he will forever be my super hero not just a mother's story

One of my life's most significant stories ends with that chapter, but it is not even remotely the entirety of my story. I found it apt to mention my struggle as a mother because I anticipate many people who pick up my book will deal with having kids of their own. My life's story can resonate with a diverse range of people, including mothers, people with anxiety, those who are bipolar or know someone who is, and anyone who had to struggle with his finances. And as the prologue clarifies, there's helpful content for those who grew up with parents who are less than ideal.

Motherhood is a thing that is interconnected with everything else in a mother's life. For example, when I got into cosmetology school the 1st time a friend volunteered to look after my kid (the one after my first). But when it was the first day of school, the friend was nowhere to be seen. The only way you could understand the inconvenience is if you recognize the story's subject, me, as a mother.

Going to cosmetology school was something that became and interest because i did my on hair and i figure hey might as well get my liscnese so i can be a BOSS!!!, and while I couldn't do it initially because the person who volunteered to fill my shoes in supervising my kid didn't show up, I got another chance when I moved.

Down in the south, the school was comparatively affordable, and I was dating someone, so there wasn't significant pressure on my shoulders to pull this off solo. However, when I moved with him down south, he decided to break up. As a result, I paused my cosmetology education.

You'll learn about my work with the City department back in New York, my therapy, and subsequent diagnosis. There's a lot more to my story, and even if you don't relate to everything that has happened in my life so far, you still get to consume an interesting life story that is true yet more fascinating than a lot of fiction out there.

But as you read the next portion that goes over my career and work, please remember my experiences with my mother and as a mother as they are quite relevant. My own childhood and the tribulations I went through as an adult will both explain and contextualize how I thought and acted. It will also shed sufficient light on my recovery and improvement. So while mine is more than just a mother's story, it still is a story featuring a mother.

what is work

Anytime friends get together after a while, they're likely to ask each other, "what do you do?" This, of course, refers to one's profession, and since working is so integral to modern life, it is often hard to separate it from one's identity. When you say, "I am a doctor," you're telling people your job while also expressing your identity.

When it is hard to identify yourself in any other way, work-life balance can become quite tough. My mother's relationship with her work might have contributed to how I handled my work. I worked for City of New York and wasn't the happiest person on the team. The supervisor seemed to target me personally. After about a year I received a new supervisor. Can you say excited welp that didnt last long because that supervisor had her issues too boy oh boy i can't catch a break. But what i can say is that i showed up to work with a smile on my face and continued to have my Hakuna Matata attitude.

In the chapter about my mother, you'll learn that she had a very authoritarian method of raising kids, and I developed a distaste for it around my highschool age. Needless to say, I wasn't the supervisor's favorite when it came to my own work life.

Fortunately, the department had a union, and when I needed time off, I was able to lean on the union for guidance. Sometimes factors align perfectly for you to go where you are meant to go. And this time, I was meant to walk out of that job.

You can tell by now that I'm not the type to seek pity. I don't ask for it and definitely don't value it. So I've kept many of my struggles to myself. But bottling those up can lead to certain passive-aggressive behaviors or even lead to a meltdown. Thankfully nothing so theatrical happened. But there has been times where …… wellllll…… yeah that's a story for another time LOL

Still, I remember looking at the scanner and wanting to throw it at my supervisor. One of my coworkers noticed that I was really struggling with my emotions. Since the colleague knew my story, they were empathetic enough to suggest I take a break and go smoke a cigarette. Eventually, they suggested I go to the union and express what I have been dealing with at work as well as some other personal things that i was dealing with . Whie there i spoke with somebody and from what i told them they determined that i should speak with the Psychologists .It was recomended for me to take medical leave and to begin therpay. It was there that i was diagnosed as being severely depressed, having serve anxiety and bipolar disorder. Yeah that was a lot

This happened a while back, and even to this day, well-intentioned people are working to remove the stigma from therapy. Back then, asking someone to see a therapist was seen as an insult. But because the coworker who brought it up seemed to have empathy, I took the idea seriously and spoke to somebody at the union .But I will not lie, at least fifty percent of the motivation was to get away from work. Still, I went in with an open mind and willing to accept help, and if there's anything I want to convey in this chapter, it is that if you need support, there's no harm in seeing a therapist. And if you get therapy, please don't do so defensively. I was initially a bit skeptical but learned the therapy's true value in just a few sessions. So, you should keep an open mind and be prepared to learn something about yourself that you didn't know.

knowing myself

I started this book by talking about how my mother's attitude resulted in certain behaviors in me. This was far from a spontaneous realization. I wasn't as lucid about how my upbringing affected me as one would assume from reading this book. That's because most of the sober insight injected throughout was accumulated during therapy.

I believe leaving my job with the City of New York was one of the best things to happen to me because it led to therapy. Here, I learned many things about myself. Noting them all down might not be interesting or valuable, but I will point out a few reactions that you might spot in your own life.

I was diagnosed as bipolar, and this came as a little bit of a surprise to me. I had previously seen depictions of bipolar people in the media and couldn't relate any of them to myself. Please do not use the internet, television, or film to self-diagnose because what is shown in media is quite removed from reality.

I had thought bipolar meant being very sweet and switching to very angry real quick. It isn't as simple as that. Being bipolar is more nuanced and has to do with perspective and attention switching between two opposing viewpoints. While one might act extremely hot and cold because of being bipolar, it is not the disorder in its entirety.

I learned to handle my anxiety. One of the key realizations I had in therapy was that I was naturally more open to negative emotion compared to the average. In other words, for me to be calm in the same situation as my friends, I had to put in more effort. In hindsight, this makes me proud because I've gone through tougher situations than most of my colleagues, ex-classmates, friends, and family yet have persevered despite having severe anxiety.

At a period in my life, I was extremely depressed as well. While this wasn't exactly postpartum depression, it had to do with the cocktail of uncertainty and a lack of security. This, alongside constant comparisons and the need to be good while simultaneously defying authority, created a scattered mix of contradictions that led to my depression.

As my story progresses, you'll see how I overcame these internal obstacles and battled these invisible demons. But one of the most rewarding things to come out of therapy was how I dismantled the imaginary monster I had built up out of someone who was only human with good and bad like the rest of us: my mother.

my mother and I

My mother and I were pretty close for the most part. when i was younger like elementary school junior high young. My earliest memories involve a lot of absence from her side due to her being at work and going to school at night, Then came highschool. I remember some shouting matches where I wasn't even shouting. These one-way yelling contests seemed unfair enough for me to think my mom was a jerk. And I had carried this opinion for quite a while. I grew up remembering how alcohol was the demonic influence that turned my mother into this hurtful person.

But in therapy, I discovered a side I had not paid a lot of attention to. I was still seeing my mother from the eyes of a child who couldn't understand adult problems. In therapy, I learned to look back at things while incorporating my adult experience into the mix. My mother wasn't a monster; she was human. And just like every human, she had her negatives and her positives.

I looked back and asked myself, was my mom a bad mother? Not at all. She was a very hard-working woman, and she made sure she did everything she could with what she had. Her absence may have triggered abandonment issues in me, but she had to be out to work so we could live.

She worked with New York City's ACS (Administration for Child Services). Her job involved visiting different homes to make sure the children were fine. She would give stern warnings to people if they were slacking and even had to move children from home to home. I can recall days where she didn't just have to visit homes in a different state but had to actually drive kids from home from one state to another.

Thankfully, most of the work was within the area we lived in. Once, she was talking to a colleague or a neighbor and brought up a case where she took someone's children away. I asked her if she really took people's kids away. She nodded.

Then I asked her why they were so glad to see her. She then explained that even though she took children away, it was the last resort. And I can now remember times when she packed up stuff like food and clothes to help families keep their kids. She went out of her way to make sure that the children had a great life.

However, her work bled into her personal life, and she found comfort in alcohol and drugs . That became the undoing of our home environment. Only after therapy was I able to acknowledge that she had her flaws and her virtues and that I was, to some degree, a product of both. I also decided that I didn't have to be a product of my upbringing. Since then, I've held on to my mother's perseverance and added a layer of my own stoic analysis to my life's decisions.

parenting and personhood

My greatest issue with my mom comes from my high school days. While she had accumulated experience in how to manage children's upbringing and see whether kids were physically abused or not taken care of properly, she had built a checkbox system of analyzing wellbeing.

As an ACS employee, she could walk into a house and check relevant boxes before deciding whether a kid was better off there or somewhere else. Some of these boxes include the following.

- the kid is receiving sufficient food
- the child is not physically harmed
- the child has access to sufficient clothing
- the child is not sexually abused

Such qualifiers can tell whether a child is being raised appropriately to some degree. But these boxes don't account for emotional torture, verbal abuse, and disregard of personhood. And my mother didn't recognize the harm of these intangibles.

While she never beat me up, There were a couple of times where things got a bit hectic tho, she would literally yell at me, and that became quite prominent around my high school years. That's because she wanted to instill discipline with authority, and I was becoming my own person around the same time.

Her parenting positioned discipline at odds with me being my own person. As a result, I would Try to speak my mind or speak on my feelings and get yelled at. This bred in me to stay quite, to keep how im feeling to myslef because it might make someone mad, So in turn when i finally became a grown up when another adult would be overly agressive with me i wasnt with it. Had I not realized this in therapy, I would have been perpetually insubordinate and would never have held a job in any organization with a hierarchical structure.

Most companies have a hierarchy, and even CEOs are answerable to others. Now I understand that not every supervisor, manager, or leader, is a clone of my mother asking me to "shut up and do the thing." It still makes me laugh how in my younger years, I used to tell my mom I would never go to college because I didn't want to be away from her. Perhaps it was because of scarcity, for she wasn't around all the time.

However, by the time I was in 10th grade, I couldn't wait to leave for college. I asked myself what I was thinking when I expressed disinterest in going away. If you're a parent reading this, please recognize that emotional abuse and yelling at your kids can also leave scars. Learn to respect their personhood and switch to discourse-oriented parenting.

It might require more patience to explain things to your children but get their will on your side instead of crushing it with your authority. The moment your children start seeing your authority as their enemy is when you lose them. And if you've had a parent who imposed himself or herself like that, you need to recognize their behavior's impact on yourself, so you can avoid lashing out at authority.

discourse-oriented parenting

As mentioned in the prologue, one of my goals with this book is to make sure you get value out of reading my story. I know that you're reading this instead of watching a reality show or gossiping about other people, and it would be a pleasure if reading my life's story leads to a valuable change in your life. One way to positively impact your home environment is to shift from authority-centric parenting to discourse-oriented parenting.

For the longest time, humanity was ruled by forceful kings, but the leaders who persevered were the ones installed with the love of their public instead of its fear. When even kings realize that they can't keep people perpetually terrified, how can you expect your children to remain disciplined by the threat of your dominance?

Discourse-oriented parenting is inconvenient. It is hard enough to raise a child with standard parenting, and most of us don't want the added burden of holding dialogues with our children when instilling discipline into them. But once you are used to this, you'll no longer need to constantly monitor your kids for them to be good; they'll be good in your absence.

More importantly, they'll want to be around you. There's something called likability bias that governs a lot of human decision-making. It basically means that people will rationalize a lot of things done by a person they like. That is why you can often see people defending their favorite politician for doing the same things they criticize the opposing politician for doing. So how do you make use of likability bias? By being a likable parent. When you're a fun parent, your kids want to be good just because it pleases you.

If this idea appeals to you, then follow these principles to be a more discourse-oriented parent.

Make it undoubtable, that you have their best interest at heart.
It might be obvious to you that you care about your children above all else, but they don't know that. In fact, even knowing it cerebrally isn't enough. You have to show them how much you care to the point that it becomes a

core belief. If you skip this step, you'll spend hours convincing them that each rule you invoke is for their benefit, but if your kids understand that you care about them, they'll self-explain your rules as being necessary for their well-being.

Have patience
The second principle of dialogue-oriented parenting is that you can't rush your kids to perfection. Your children will be naughty for a while, and that's okay; the world doesn't punish kids for making mistakes the way it punishes adults. Your job is not to make them perfect but to teach them how to conduct themselves well enough as adults. So be patient as you explain the benefits of behaving properly, getting educated, and being polite.

Use Jedi mind tricks.
Finally, the best way to get your child to behave properly is to let him come to the conclusion himself. Don't hand rules down but instead ask them loaded questions till they come to the appropriate answer. This way, they'll not intrinsically reject anything coming from you. And by mastering this step, you will ensure that your kids don't stonewall you.

contextualizing authority

There are two types of people reading this chapter right now: ones who made notes while reading the last chapter and ones who skipped it without reading past the first paragraphs. If you skipped the last chapter, chances are you're quite far from parenthood. You could be a young adult who doesn't plan to have kids anytime soon or just someone who doesn't want kids whatsoever.

Either way, it is essential that you look back and ponder whether your parents were authoritative in their parenting-style. If they were, then you have likely developed a bad relationship with authority.

Overbearing parents can lead to two types of people. The majority of the children grow up to lash out against any type of authority. A small percentage become perpetually submissive. Neither of those options is particularly nice because authority is neither an inherent virtue nor a threat. You should, therefore, contextualize authority.

Authority must not erase individuality.
Regardless of whether it is the authority of a parent or an employer, it should never intrude upon your individuality. Even the fact that you show up at your office is decided by you as an individual out of self-interest. You have a contract or an agreement that you have willingly entered. When you submit to authority unconditionally, you may lose your individuality, and that can lead to self-destructive behavior.

Authority must be accepted with self-interest.
Even as a child, you should accept your parents' authority because it is good for you. If your parents, for an extreme example, ask you to sell drugs, you should reject their authority. Of course, as a grown-up, you should respect this principle as well. Many people reject all authority indiscriminately, and I would say that should only happen if it is objectively the best thing for them. However, they usually end up losing jobs, friends, and social standing in the process.

Ask these questions

From my story, one can see my initial relationship with authority and how I was uber-defensive. Eventually, I learned to take a step back and view authority as a tool. If it helps me or my mission, I'll go along, and if it doesn't, I will take a stand. The following questions will help you decide whether you should respect authority in a given situation or not.

- Is this person's authority a threat to my individual principles?
- Would the world be objectively better if every one of my peers rejected this person's authority?
- Is there anything I gain from obeying this person?
- Is what I gain from obeying this person worth what I give away in terms of my personal freedom?

moving down south

Some stereotypes are associated with moving down south: that you grow around your belly, life gets calmer, and you build friendships that last forever. This wouldn't be an interesting story if everything went as expected. While I moved to North Carolina for a specific set of reasons, almost all of them eluded me when I went down there. Throughout the next couple of chapters, I'll detail how inconvenient my time in North Carolina was initially, and you may wonder why I put up with any of it, to begin with.

That's why I must clarify my motivation behind the move. As you may recall from earlier chapters, I wanted to get a house so I could move my son in. In New York, most Landlords weren't willing to put up with the kind of modifications required to shift him to the same unit like the one I was occupying. More importantly, there just wasn't enough space since I wasn't a C-suite executive with a six-figure income.

In North Carolina, I could get a house and the rent would cheaper, ,and the amount of space i would have would be amazng Holding things down isn't too hard if you land the right job. This IF is quite a big IF. But hindsight is 2020. I actually didn't know how much rides on being in the right environment and having the right paycheck.

But before I delve deeper into the problems I faced when I initially moved here, I have to further explain my drivers. My second driver for this shift was my own mental health. You know by now that I'm quite an anxious person. On top of that, I wasn't just in any city; I was in New York. Even the quietest burrow in the state is busier than North Carolina's busiest spot.

My mother had moved down to North Carolina 15 years ago and was my only reference point for what I assumed was life down south. That was my biggest mistake as I was listening to an unreliable narrator. My mother was motivated to get me down there, and in her conversations, she made settling down in the south seem pretty easy. It was no one's fault that I bought it. I had lived most my life with her and should have known better, but when you see no way out of a stressful situation, you airbrush the one exit you see. I didn't want to be alone, and I wanted to have my son with me. Unfortunately, neither of those things ended up happening.

At this point, you may think I didn't have anyone living with me, and that's why I say I felt alone. But in reality, I was in a crowded house with my partner and my other kid. I just felt alone because I saw no sign of people caring for me on a human level. The company, it turns out, isn't about physical proximity. It is about empathy.

crowded alone

Before I moved to North Carolina, I had started dabbling in spirituality. Thanks to the internet and Barnes an Nobels I had access to educational material. My spiritual studies had made me more sensitive to the energies of those around me. I have always been the person who paid attention to people's vibes.

When I first came to North Carolina, I was with my boyfriend at the time and my kid(not his kid but might as well be his kid he has been around since my son was 8 months old. When we moved down south my son was 7years old . My first son still needed critical care and was in New Jersey at a hospital where he was on consistent life-support. My move would help lay the foundation to bring him closer to me.

For the moment, I was in between my mother's house and the house i worked at.. Yes, the overbearing shadow I had escaped and fought so hard to seek independence from had found its way to impose itself over my life. On the phone, she had told me she would help me by first giving me a job, and soon, I'd have enough saved up to move out and maybe even get a different job. She made it all sound so easy.

What job was she going to give me? Well, I was going to be assisting in running her boarding house for people with mental health problems. She wasn't running a group home, but it was pretty close to that. She gave clients a roof over their heads, essential care, and even cooked food for them. That was before we moved there. Since our move, we began taking up these chores. Along with helping to take care of some older family memebers

My boyfriend, my son, and I used to live in one room; then there was my maternal grandmother and her mother who would live in the next room and my maternal Grandpa stayed in the room across from those two boy are they hilarious. , and on the other side of the house, there were six clients residing. Two of them were in one room and the rest in a bigger room.

My boyfriend would wake up and cook breakfast for the house. I would get my boy ready in the meantime and, after breakfast, drop him at the bus stop from where he would go to school. He socialized with people there.

When my boyfriend got a job, he got to socialize there, but I felt alone. I didn't know anyone here, and I wasn't in a position to go out and socialize. First of all, I didn't know how to drive. Moreover, I was not free to even go down to the store that wasnt to far from the place i worked/lived at all. And that's where my anxiety started to bubble back up. They say humans can survive any conditions as long as they see an out. But if they can't see a way out, they panic. My mental energy and spirit were off balance.

control and care

Control and care go hand in hand. That might be an odd statement for many but is true in the context of parent and child. When your children are young, you want a greater degree of control because you care about them. When your children don't know any better, it is your responsibility to make sure they make the right choices. You can't have an hour-long debate about your child to convince them not to touch a hot pan. You have to command them not to, and they have to obey you.

However, children soon develop the ability to think for themselves. Parents who don't want to give up control, though, convince themselves they still know what's better for the children. With this rationale, they continue to crush their children's spirits. Many readers may know such a parent. Even some boyfriends, girlfriends, and spouses can be like that.

In my opinion, any adult who tries to control another's behavior with the rationale of compassion is only using empathy as an excuse to gain power. And if parents do this with their grown-up kids, you can be sure they were controlling because of their own needs and never the needs of their children.

My mother crafted an entire strategy to expand her control over my life. She started by taking control of my finances. As my employer, she was the one who paid. I mean she be meaning well jus go about it wrong in my opinion, thankfully she connected me to healthcare ancgey because there would be no way i would have been able to survive on what she was giving . I wasnt really feeling the job i had But this could be fixed: all I had to do was get another job. She made sure that I couldn't do that. She kept me occupied at all times, and since I didn't know how to drive, I could not even get away without her driving me.

    According to my mother, someone always had to be with the clients,my great grandmother and my grandpa so when I would want to go somewhere and need a ride most the time it was an issue. I asked her to teach me how to drive, and she asked me to get specific permits first. And when I got the right permit, she never had the time to teach me. This made me realize that her other promise regarding helping me find a therapist would similarly go nowhere.

That's why I did my own research and found a therapist. My mother would have to drive me there and then drive me back. The reason being my anxiety. I wasn't able to stand in even a semi-crowded bus. Since my mother was driving, she made sure I knew it was going to be on her terms. While session times made it impossible for her to get her way with when she was going to drop me at the therapist's, she applied her will on the way back: by taking me to NA meetings.

Issues and Issues

Some of my readers may assume that I hate my mother. I do not. I understand her circumstances and how she developed the personality she developed, but I also find it important, to be honest. I care more about being authentic than I do about appearing good. When my mother was exerting herself on my individuality, I had negative emotions regarding her habits.

And while it is important to signify what I felt in those moments, it is also important to lend perspective that balances the picture. My mother had raised us while working a tough job. And since she became a workaholic, she assumed it to be the natural state of being. As a result, she didn't notice that she was harming my mental health by pushing me to be on all the time.

Corporations spend millions of dollars getting their employees certain benefits. Perks include free trips, all-expenses-paid staycations, and playrooms at the headquarters. Do you think they do this out of goodwill? Of course, not! The reason corporations spend money keeping their employees happy and entertained is because that's good for business in the long run.

Many small business owners don't understand this. As a result, you have people like my mom who wouldn't notice the fact that working where I lived was keeping me in a constant work-mode and that I needed an outlet. I still admire her for overcoming her drug problems, but I had no interest in sitting through NA meetings when I couldn't relate to anything being said there.

One day, I told my mother I was going to take the bus back from therapy. I didn't know I could, but I had to try. My boyfriend stayed with me on the phone throughout the trip, and by talking to him, I could keep myself calm. I had anxiety problems and was scared of using public transport in a new place.

But between her issues and mine, mine were the only ones I could do something about. I want to encourage you to see each point of conflict with this perspective. Ask yourself what the other party's issues are and what issues you have. And then disregard what they can do to make things better: ask yourself what you can do. That will give you more power and prestige. It takes one small step, and before you know it, momentum is carrying you forward.

While breaking the bus-riding barrier was a pivotal point in establishing my life in North Carolina, it didn't feel like that at the time. I was still living with an overbearing mom who tried her best to keep me dependent. It is quite interesting how very little had changed compared to my high school days.

a throwback about throwing back

If you've browsed social media hashtags on a Thursday, you have probably come across the term "throwback Thursday." Platforms have come and gone, but the hashtag remains evergreen. IT is like Taco Tuesdays, a persistent phenomenon. Throwback refers to a real-life flashback. When you bring back old content, you are essentially throwing back to the time it first originated.

Since we are talking about my mother's attitude, when I moved down South, it is only apt to throw back to the time in high school where she was keeping me from going out. She had made it a habit to yell and scream at me, and that wasn't good for my self-esteem. There was this one time at band camp lol nah but this one time I came in the house 3mins late yes 3mins late in the afternoon yup thats right . and when i say she was tight with me you would have thought we had somewhere important to be and i was making us late. She was going off off I told her I didnt understand what the issue was. Of couse in her eyes i was being disrespectful by speaking at this point in my life i as about 17 years old i told my mom i was going to my cousin's house because alot was happening and i really wsnt trying to go thruogh all of this .

She physically blocked my path. Stood in front of my bedroom door She said that if I was going to go out, it was going to be through her. I didn't want to hit, shove or push my own mother. So I simply jumped over the couch and slipped past her. During the time, I had lemonade braids.

These braids were popularized by Beyonce in her album Lemonade. But this was long before the album was released. Still, I had long braids (butt-length), and my mother grabbed hold of them and yanked me back towards herself. Since she didn't treat me like her child at that moment, I too turned and fought her like I would any person attacking me.

When my brother came out, he started yelling, "Victoria , what are you doing? Why are you hitting mom." My mom called, 911 and the police took me To my Granny's house. My friends at school were wondering where I was, and I had to return with a story that didn't paint me like someone who assaulted their own mother. But in the long run, everyone figured out the kind of overbearing presence she had.

In my first few months in North Carolina, I didnt have much contact with as many people in New York as i thought i would have but nowadays, I'm better connected to my friends. My friends helped keep me sane while first adjusting even still till this day. I knew having friends was important, But it wasnt until i wasnt around them on a daily that i realised how much i needed them. Most of them ask, "Victoria, is your mother still like that." Sadly, I have to say "yes." You cannot change people against their will.

If you learn anything from this chapter, it is that you cannot change people. People may change if they are inspired by you, but you cannot change their personalities. You can only decide what you're willing to put up with. Abusive people can reign in their abuse if you fight back, but ultimately, they possess the same psyche and, therefore, will do whatever they can to get back to the old dynamic.

While my mother is far from a case of classic abuse, her controlling nature reemerged in my adulthood despite her being sweet and understanding on the phone. The moment I reached North Carolina, she was not the same person as the one on the phone: she was the person who made my highschool days unbearable.

attempting to adjust

By now, you can tell that my move to North Carolina had led me to an inconvenient lifestyle. I wasn't able to get away from the work-stay relationship I had developed with my mother. When I started going to therapy (or at least coming back from it) without her support, she took it personally. When taking the bus to the therapist's place, I would have to go an hour earlier.

If you take buses often, you understand why. Firstly, the bus doesn't go directly to your destination. Secondly, you need to hedge against the possibility that the bus might get held up at different stops. When I informed my mother that I would need to go an hour earlier, she said she would need another worker to come down for the hour and that I would need to pay them.

On paper, this might work but not in the context of a normal job. I told my mom that employees don't get penalized for their medical issues. It reminded me of how I got started in therapy, to begin with. Ironically, I "went along" with therapy back in New York because I wanted to get away from work. And though I entered therapy with skepticism and defensiveness, I soon realized how much I needed it.

Even upon moving to North Carolina, I was in touch with my therapist in the city before I found one in the region. Nowadays, with apps like BetterHelp, one can have remote access to a therapist, but such platforms were in their infancy when I was trying to get help. To my mother, therapy was just enabling my dramatic personality.

To her, I was just dramatic. The problem with my mother's insistence on everything being her way was that if she did not acknowledge your issues, then the solutions to your issues were complete nonsense to her. Imagine having diabetes and asking the only person who can go to the pharmacy to get you some insulin. How would you feel if the person said insulin was a scam and that you were just dramatic? It isn't even about feelings; it is about survival.

I did my best to adjust but had soon concluded that I had to move out. As scary as it was in a place where you barely knew anyone, I had to put myself out there in order to live outside of my mother's dictatorship. And as if my internal courage was linked to reality itself, my resolve manifested a client who lived thirty minutes away. Out of twenty-four hours, I had earned one hour of freedom.

double the loneliness

I felt that even if I had issues with my mother, I still was among family. But then I started having trouble with my partner. My initial goal was to build a life with him and my kids, but then things started looking shaky. It started with small lies. As they say, communication is the foundation of strong relationships; I say honesty is the strength of all foundations.

When the lies started misleading people regarding bills and cash, my family started treating him poorly. I would say the punishment wasn't proportionate to the "crime." While he was irresponsible with finances and transparency, my mother was downright cruel in moments where we needed her.

I still remember how bad it felt calling her up to ask for a ride and her response was that he should be able to get a bus if he doesn't have money for uber. IT doesn't matter how wrong your partner has been; hearing your family talk like that about them can't ever feel good.

For now, my family was disappointed in him, but eventually, I too got disappointed. I will cover that in a later chapter. What matters is that this friction took its toll on the relationship and resulted in our initial distance from each other.

While we hadn't broken up yet, I started feeling even lonelier because I couldn't rely on my boyfriend either. A big part of your relationship is the fact that no matter what happens, you can count on each other. But the tragedy of my situation was that I could count only on the good intentions of both my mother and my partner but couldn't rely on the methods of either one.

When you're in a position in life where you can't rely on anyone, the last thing you want is for a situation to occur where people's reliability is tested. This is best explained with an analogy. If you are in a boat and can't trust the lifejacket, the last thing you want to see is a hole in the boat's hull. Well, that is what happened in my life. I knew I could not rely on my mother's charitable nature and a part of me knew my boyfriend wasn't going to be the responsible person when I need him to be, then I got word that my son had passed away in the New Jersey hospital.

losing your why

You know that I had moved down to North Carolina with the hopes of living with my son. My son had been my "why" for a lot of things. I had stuck to work duties I didn't like because of my son. And out of my love for him, I had returned to the overbearing fold of my mother despite being independent since the age of 17.

On April 3, 2018, my son passed away. Learning that he had passed away first took me off the planet. I could not accept that this had happened despite knowing that every year he was living was a year more than medical professionals had expected. He was born with a zero-year life expectancy, but he was a fighter. After some hours had passed, reality crept back into my consciousness. I had to figure out my way back to New York so I could attend his funeral.

In the meantime, I had to get a break from work. My boyfriend said he was going to pay the phone bill, and my mother said I could take time off. This was comforting, but I had a feeling that neither of these declarations would materialize.

When I came home the phone was off. Everything should have been on point, my partner should have made sure of it, but alas, he didn't. More importantly, I had no time to grieve. While my son passed away on the 3rd, I was back in North Carolina on the 7th due to the rigidity of my employer's demands. She kept saying she had to get back to her business ok but what does that have to do with me is all i thought i wanted to stay longer I wanted to stay where i felt the love in NYC were my friends were

I don't even call her my mother when narrating that part because she acted too selfishly. My needs were ignored at different periods of my life, but this was that one instance that just broke my heart. Not only was I putting up with so many complications, but I was doing so for no reason. I had lost my why.

I couldn't live with my son down in the south now. I could not find an escape for my mental wellbeing either. My residence in North Carolina was more stressful than my life in New York. In New York, the city might be busy, but there was solitude at home. Here, there was no boundary between work and life, and the flow was one way. Work stress would creep into my personal life, but the empathy of personal relationships never made way into work considerations. I had had enough.

fed-up value

I think there's a lot of value in getting fed up. People do not realize the importance of the breaking point. When I had had enough of my situation, I stopped looking at how others were disappointing me. I decided it was time to take charge and do for myself what I had ignored.

All my life, I had done things for others and gotten disappointed when my feelings and situation weren't considered. But how can I blame my mother for not thinking about me when I didn't think about myself either? I had always wanted to be in a creative field, yet I ignored my calling three separate times. At first, it was because my mother said I would be a starving artist selling paintings by the side of the road so i stayed at a college i really no longer wanted to be at but i got my degree thats the important part right?

The next time, I had gotten prematurely disheartened when a friend didn't show up to look after my kid on the first day of school.
The third time I stated Cosmetology school in North Carolina and I couldn't continue with my cosmetology education because i got suspened from school for something i didn't even do smh. Some dumb dumb ,sweet baby unicorns not even gona start that story cause its jus gonna ugggh lol. And the fourth time sheesh ,My partner had broken up with me so had to pick up more hours at work and that was the last time i was going to be putting my deams on hold . by that time i was able to get a job at a gas station while going to school, to help out with the bills I didn't even pause to protest with the universe how unfair things were.

My interest in spirituality had blossomed further. My therapy began to move me forward as well. I was more rational with my choices and took things less personally. That is why you can see me love my mother from a distance and understand why she is the way she is. Clearly, that wasn't how things were, to begin with.

What I want to emphasize is that my life has been quite cyclical up until I had enough. In your life, you need to figure out which things are running on a loop. If you understand what you dislike about your patterns, you can induce a breaking point where you have no choice but to move forward.

In my life, I was constantly ignoring myself, and anytime I did things for myself, I would abandon them halfway through at the first sign of someone else needing my help. In certain cases, this was inevitable: I could not ignore my kids for my own sake, but from a spiritual perspective: it was self-induced. I was inviting the universe to take me away from serving myself.

I was tired of being disappointed, controlled, and manipulated. And when I had enough, and I released my "no more" declaration into the universe, things started to snap into place. Even painful things happened. But they were essential. I was done with getting lied to, but maybe I didn't have the courage to walk away from my relationship. Life took my boyfriend out anyway. He walked out of his own accord. I had enough with my mother controlling me, and soon my finances weren't tied to her practice. I had found freedom. But more importantly, I had found what I wanted to do with my freedom.

mind, body, spirit

As I mentioned, I had dabbled in spirituality long before my son passed, but when I lost him, everything I was doing became temporarily pointless. My move down south was to be closer to him. And when everything that had to do with money, location, and relationships lost its purpose, spirituality seemed to be the only thing that had meaning. And during that period, I got more interested in chakras, healing, and manifestation and Crystals

Lisa Nichols served as a beacon of light: her content was enlightening and her story inspiring. As I learned more about different ways to cultivate spirituality in my life, things started to work out. I was in a better mental state than before. Even my finances worked out. I had gotten skinnier after moving to North Carolina (something one would consider impossible). Now I gained back enough to be at a healthy weight.

Everything was falling into place in my life; then, I had a gnawing feeling. I was so used to focusing on others that focusing on myself was making me feel guilty. But I noticed that as I paid attention to myself, the lives of those I loved got better. I was able to better provide for my child and be there for him more. How my life turned out taught me one thing about parenting: don't do it at the cost of yourself.

My mother had worked so hard for us that she had built resentment and an intense need to be compensated. That's human nature, according to Robert Greene and Jordan Peterson. If you ignore your own well-being for your kids, you will burden them with an unhealthy parent. Now that I had made peace with putting myself first while caring about those around me, I wanted to go out and spread the message. This time, I was going to help others but not at the cost of myself. I was going to help others while helping myself. And that's where the idea of spiritual problem-solving emerged.

From my life's story, you can see that spirituality didn't seem to be a priority because life's challenges had occupied my attention. And the moment I embraced my spiritual side, my mind and body clicked, and the surrounding reality became better. In your life, too, you may have overlooked or ignored spirituality. Even if you don't get to work with me one-on-one or in a group to find your personal path to using spirituality as medicine for your life's material ailments, I encourage you to look into as much spiritual literature as is possible. It is your duty to overcome your problems because we can't keep passing the mess down to the next generation.

epilogue

Congratulations on completing this book. You have learned more about dealing with overbearing parents, fostering independence, managing anxiety, and discourse-oriented parenting. I have written my story in a way that educates its readers on a subconscious level. So please read this book at different times in your life. Each time, you will find different insights because different parts of my story will resonate with you. You can read this as a mother, a child, a newcomer to a different workplace or state, or as someone dealing with mental health issues. Once again, I thank you for taking an interest in my story, and I leave you with the following words until the next time:

Often, it is the hard thing that is the right thing to do.

www.ingramcontent.com/pod-product-compliance
Lightning Source LLC
LaVergne TN
LVHW031616060526
838201LV00008B/191